RUMORS OF SHORE

Poems by
Paul Fisher

BLUE LIGHT PRESS ❖ 1ST WORLD PUBLISHING

1ˢᵗ WORLD
PUBLISHING

SAN FRANCISCO ❖ FAIRFIELD ❖ DELHI

WINNER OF THE 2009 BLUE LIGHT BOOK AWARD

RUMORS OF SHORE
Copyright ©2010 by Paul Fisher

1ST WORLD LIBRARY
106 South Court Street
Fairfield, Iowa 52556
www.1stworldpublishing.com

BLUE LIGHT PRESS
1563 45th Avenue
San Francisco, California, 94122

BOOK AND COVER ART / DESIGN
Melanie Gendron
www.melaniegendron.com

AUTHOR PHOTO
Linda Fisher

FIRST EDITION

LCCN: 2010928104

ISBN: 9781421891491

Acknowledgments

The author wishes to gratefully acknowledge the periodicals and anthologies in which many of these poems originally appeared, sometimes in earlier versions:

Beauty/Truth: a Journal of Ekphrastic Poetry: "Village of the Mermaids"
Cave Wall: "Tunnel Vision"
The Centrifugal Eye: "Ghost," "Middle Age," "The Petrified Wife,"
   "Sasquatch Speaks," "Shapeshifter," "The Sun Again," "Tyger Burning"
The Christian Science Monitor: "Blue Whale"
Defined Providence: "Irregularities in the White"
DMQ Review: "North of the Crater," "Winter Geese"
The Dirty Napkin: "Dream of the Savanna," Dream Water,"
   "Elegy for a Border Collie"
Edgz: Conversations at the Borderland: "Dream of the Pacific,"
   "The Return"
Explorations: "Old Story"
Innisfree Poetry Journal: "The Gift," "Local Idiom," "Nowhere"
Kakalak 2009 Anthology of Carolina Poets: "The Butcher's Dream"
Lunarosity: "The Moon you are Creating," "To a Slinky"
Mannequin Envy: "After Looking at a Facsimile of Leonardo's Journals,"
   "Take Magritte"
OVS Magazine: "Blackberry House," "Drought," "To a Pawned Guitar"
Passager: "Archaeology," "Kindergarten: 1945"
The Pedestal Magazine: "To My Left Hand"
The 2010 Poet's Guide to New Hampshire: "Lucky Star"
The Portland Oregonian: "Beaverton, Oregon Blues"
Slow Trains: "Sleeping on Amtrak," "The Sofa on Mount Everest"
Snow Monkey: "Letter to a Lost Brother," "Thirst"
The Sow's Ear Poetry Review: "The Well"
Terrain.org: A Journal of the Built & Natural Environments: "Inland Sea,"
   "At the Symphony"
Umbrella Journal: "Red," "Midnight in the Garden," "Stick Man,"
   "String Theory"
Waccamaw Journal: "The Boat," "Jonah"
WordWrights: "Fear," "Domestication," "Running in D.C."

CONTENTS

II

III

FOR LINDA

Art urges voyages—
and it is easier to stay at home.

—Gwendolyn Brooks

The Boat

Maybe the eyes of a dragon or goddess
glare from its prow.

More likely it leaks, loses an oar,
and reeks of rainbows awash on a sheen
of gutted salmon and gasoline.

If it's a liner, we lash ourselves
to whatever will float or sell.

No matter which. We choose. We're aboard,
icebergs or no, as we plow
through the songs of the siren stars—

one boat, black water, dark whispering below.

I.

JONAH

The whale welcomed me,
tongue meadow-rough, glossy
grin encompassing oceans,
black hole swallowing
promises, memory, gods.
O monstrous belly,
what alchemy occurred
before you spit my half-
digested self,
bone, blood, phlegm and shit
transformed, somewhere
among the galaxies,
without rudder, sail or oar,
between septillion stars, one life-
line spun from prayer?

ORIGINAL THIRST

Sometimes you fill your heart up
with silence, then plunge
with your other heart down
through crusts of ghost-riddled strata
to inundated hollows of sound.

You listen without breath
to the pause before thunder, to the well-
tuned tap of a thousand water clocks.

You hear the heartbeat of oceans,
the raga, the renga, the unceasing prayer.
You quench your original thirst,
then reach for sweet goblets of air.

The Well

Dig anywhere.
You'll find
something.
Move enough
dirt, and you're
sure to strike
rock. Lower
yourself. Earth
is your true
divining rod.
Then, if you
let your eyes
follow the
creaking bucket
all the way
up the wet
black rope,
you'll discover
again what a
steep and
slender hole
the hard
stars fill.

DREAM WATER

Sunk in a dream of water,
you can hold your breath

as long as you want,
or breathe as deep as you dare.

You're amazed that white
light plumbs so far,

that candlefish halos orbit
auras of tangled hair.

You could float or fly,
but choose to walk

beyond undulating timberlines
of unkempt kelp.

There, among ghost coral's
skeletal cells, you learn

how the sea transforms itself
into rain, into forest, into lovers,
into salt.

Dream of the Pacific

"Look west at the hill of water:
it is half the planet."
                    —*Robinson Jeffers*

Drawn by ocean to Oregon bluffs,
I lie at the edge of a wave-torn headland,
caught between roots of a toppled Douglas fir.

Face it, I tell myself,
dream waters rake every shore;
logs leveled one day end up upended another.

I stare down the war-like Pacific—
one way to conjure disaster.
I straddle cliffs, pace mineral decks,

pilot dune-trapped wrecks
burying, then unburying themselves—
no way to escape demon weather.

After eternity times two, my mind ground
smooth as a pebble, my soul a small, ringed stone,
I begin again at the beginning—

phosphorescence unblinking,
blind oceans purring,
rich rivers nursing one ravenous half of a world.

To a Blue Whale

Sea-flanked volcano,
you erupt
beside our tiny boat.

Already drenched with mist,
we find ourselves
rechristened
by the maelstrom of your breath.

Before us you loom,
barnacled island
as scarred as the moon.

Deep enough to swallow stars,
one atoll eye stares up.
Tsunami song explodes.
Flukes upend.

Your continent sounds.

INLAND SEA

Carried below by mudslides, forest may stand
a thousand years, preserved beneath frigid
waters of the sound.
　　　　　　—Oceans Review

Around eight o'clock, when shallow
fog lifts, you sometimes glimpse shore
where memory drops off,
sometimes hear the sound of water
stumbling over rocks
as smooth and striped as planets
ground half-way from stars to dust.

Ringed by trembling hills,
the Salish carved war canoes
from cedar, fire and smoke-hardened prayer.
Dogfish, crabs, gutted seals,
whatever washed belly-up on not-quite land
was pecked apart by hawks and gulls,
or fondled by a child.

Not long ago, groves launched themselves
like Yankee clippers into cold
where masts still harbor nests of owls,
cradle bones of men and wolves,
and spread blue shadows under waves
like flickering, wingless ghosts.
Silver and black, the surface is all we know—

wind caterwauling through railing and rigging,
clearing the decks of half-sunk ships.

The Coast

When I was still too young
to stutter this out, my brother dove
his P-38 into the curl of a bluff.

As small as a skipped stone's
final splash, he surfaced on time's
last page in grainy black-and-white.

The earth, once firm, surges
like an ocean; mountains morph
to waves; and everywhere I stand

rises, crests, then slides away
down a steep, eroding beach.
In fields lapping my mother's house,

I troubled the waters of boy-tall grass.
Creating surf, I drew shallows
for otters basking in kelp, depths

for the grinning crescendos of sharks.
When at last I drove myself
west to the coast, and plunged

into unending cold, night glowed.
Phosphorescence spun like a star
knocked out of orbit but ready to talk.

Breakers sounded up the spit, not
like a conch pressed to my ear,
nor like phantom bombers treading air,

but like the legend I'd learned to love,
yet never—in this life—told before.

GREENHOUSE EFFECT

To Theodore Roethke

Though we braved the same cutting rain
which coerces roses to grow,
and traveled common ruts
down peninsulas thick with spruce
toward desolate headlands and rock-strewn coasts,
I knew you only from your few, slim books.

One voice, cupped hard against my ear,
sang like a mirrored shell,
spiral facing spiral,
each chamber filled with a sea,
each sea stocked to the rim by its flickering sun.

Without a word, cloud-cover thins,
tendrils soften temples, cathedrals anchor thorns,
and the field-mouse nesting
in the quiet churchyard's corner
quakes for us all at the growl of the mower.

TYGER BURNING

for Tatiana and her mates

Run to your forest. Ask Kali
to weave you a shirt of fire, and a coat
of scattered coals.

Roll in the odor of lemongrass.
Hide among mangroves.
Be air. Be smoke. Swim among lily pads.

Flee from voices, from villagers,
from easy prey and taunting drums.
Climb the tree that is broader than Banyan,

that harbors more branches
than all the proud trees of the world.
Slip two by two into arks

built of reeds and of moonlight,
whose oars drip the fragrance of sandalwood.
May night's many temples shelter you.

Be not afraid. Though they grind your bones
and barter your head, Kali waits
among leaves and ashes,

in twilight palaces she carves for you.
Find the grove where Chital and Sambar
take their sleep.

Eat and drink till you are full.
I pray that your forests bloom darker still,
that they dream deeper dreams for Kali and for you.

ECUADOR

Out of sight
but close to sound,

midnight's jaguar
vomits bones.

Some, as smooth as dice,
cure fever.

Others, etched
like antique ivory pins,

foretell
foul weather.

Each one the doe-eyed
morning carves

into luck, luminosities,
pearls.

RED

Do not mistake me; I am no
carrot eater, no wall-eyed
nibbler at grass nor blissful
mulcher of leaves. I am what

you are taught to fear—
lion, leopard, jaguar, wolf.
From my mother's milk,
I was weaned to the hunt.

I gather bones, not straw,
to line my hut, and suffer
no flesh to wilt in my mouth.
There are two kinds of creatures,

my father said. As I quaked
in my paws, I nodded my head.

DOMESTICATION

To make your wild wolf a dog,
you must wake before dawn.

All day you must grovel
on bleeding knees and paws.

You must have the patience of a river-
torn mountain, knowing

you will need ten-thousand
dog generations.

You must sit, then heel. If you speak,
you must speak the tongue

of the bitch who suckled you.
Here is the leash. Here is the bone

etched by your father's teeth.
Good boy! Lie down! Sleep!

The Butcher's Dream

Some nights I wake from
hacking limbs, dragging
slabs of meat from hook to rack,
measuring, then slicing fat.
When I see what I have done,

I try to lay flesh back, make severed
bones mesh, close all gaps.
Sinews that hold one moment
snap the next. I curse my hands,
my stench, my craft.

To keep myself from sleep,
I scrub tables, walls, floodplain floor.
I go about my life
as morning soaks the room again
with thick, red light.

SASQUATCH SPEAKS

Born on the Ring of Fire,
in a grove the chainsaw missed,
I would have called myself a *local*
had not I-5's aromas tempted me
to taste the trembling cities
and wander faultline alleys,
my out-of-focus amble
betrayed by tabloid news.
Perhaps the village of my youth
was only a raven on a pole,
a cedar bound to clay,
whose wooden wings and once-cut roots
regrew, whose painted eyes still peer
through monkish cowls of air.
Perhaps the moon unmasked
as midnight's raven paled to wolf.
Perhaps, content to show myself,
I shed my well-worn pelt.

THE SOFA ON MOUNT EVEREST

from a dream by Mary Norbert Korte

Of course it is a purple couch
(Or should I say divan?)
at rest on Chomolungma's flank
where heart-shaped cushions
flesh the ribs
of Buddha's childhood home.
There, Yeti reclines,
doe-eyed and saying nothing,
allowing his hair to fall like snow
on velvet tundra's satin arms.
In his lap, a gift of yellow silk
which, night-by-night, the creature
shyly offers to the nun.

The Return

Wolves in the North Cascades?
Wisdom questions if it's true.
Imagination broadcasts howling packs
drowning out today's dire news.

Coyote beware!
Trapped like snow in crevices of bark,
ghost-gray tufts pronounce themselves:
Canis lupus — male.

Tracks as wide as hands mark trails
weaving through the brain's dense groves,
braiding mossy toadstool floors
with hapless mice and wimpled girls.

An image hardens in the developing room.
We glimpse a lowered head, amber eyes.
Captured by an amateur, the print reveals
only what we fear.

Neither potbellied bear nor sasquatch,
Alpha gazes from the other side,
as real as light, as palpable as blood,
as close to truth as facts dare come.

While controversy mounts in the Lamb's Heart
Bar & Grill, cubs gorge on mother's milk.
One tumbles from its den into bones,
into darkness as bright as a shield.

Into our night-ringed circle, silence spills
another hungry child.

30

LUCKY STAR

Watch the sun slip out of yellow silk,
then drape blue muslin
on its once lit self
above the town of Henniker.
There's not much else to do.

The Lucky Star's defunct,
its boisterous bar still.
A crow pecks at sunflower seed,
the only embers found.

If you have a mind to do it,
toss river rocks
off the haunted granite ledge
that looms through frozen fog.

Let boulders crack
the cold Contoocook's opaque black
and skid like curling stones
bearing down on unseen brooms.

Hike upstream
where a cloaked and hooded bridge
grasps the water's hardened edge
with wooden claws,

where ice inks intaglios
of cloven hooves and waffle soles,
bookmarks for children
whose sudden wings now fill with snow.

And if you have an appetite
for white-on-white,
for the calligraphy of mice and voles,
learn to be a wide-eyed reader,
blood-brother of the owl.

SHAPESHIFTER

Older than slate, as rippled
as the surface of a fossil lake,
found dormant on the forest floor,
slapped in irons, it escapes.

Through any window it can find,
it falls as light.
Bent on learning ways of ice,
it turns opaque, stands almost still,

mimicks boulders, logs,
chunks of broken night
inching over snowy fields
blazed subzero blue.

I've seen its shadow dance in caves
lit up behind your eyes,
on either side of silence
where it eats and drinks and lies.

LOCAL IDIOM

Zigzag through nameless woods,
I scan my skies for chimney smoke.
Like beavers that trouble our pond,
I'm comfortable closer to home.
I gnaw only edges of worlds.
When I spit them out, they caulk my lodge
and drip from its cloud-stained dome.
Threadbare firs encircle me
like a nave of blue whale ribs
while wolves chew the full mead moon
down to opalescent bone.

But I was catching other dreams
at our camp by the cold crater's rim,
the night we skipped star-stones.
A fool for you, I tossed the crumpled
wings of this poem into our fire,
then kicked at its coals
with my bare, burning feet
till embers hissed, flared, and sputtered out.
In the land of missed opportunity and stumps
where silence chants its lacquered prayer
and half the language gongs,
I ate our howling ashes – bitter in my belly,
yet sweet as stolen honey
ladled from the Great Bear's tongue.

Apology to the Muse

I wanted to erupt
through spring's litter of splinters and sticks.
Like a dew-studded seedling,
I wanted to wear the rings of wisdom
rippling the heart of a redwood tree.

Sorry I took so long. Sorry I beat
the faithful desk I owned,
overflowed my trash with tidal waves
of angry, wadded poems.

I sought shelter from wind,
blamed the storm's brackish bluster
for ripping my roots.

When slurries of mud hardened to street,
my stalk—nailed deep in asphalt earth—
wanted fistfuls of rain, a body of dirt,
your junkyard of craters
shining pointblank
above Christ-old sequoia and cured concrete.

The Gift

Searching for the lost coin,
now stubborn in its hiding,
I sweep the hardwood floor,
scour the cedar deck,
rifle drawers, claw through chests,
rake the garden's tangled depths,
mole-roads, rose roots, blackberry crypts,
corner it at last
—belly-up but breathing—
behind an empty apple box
forgotten in the dream-infested
mushroom cellar, pulsing like a toad
resigned to spit and brood
below the creaking timbers of the house.
Tiny as a redwood seed
and rough as pumice stone, it cries
with the thin voice of a penny
when I bend to pick it up,
as if by pleading in the dark
sown deep around us
it could deflect one thorn or thought,
reverse one whirling atom,
as if by sinking into shadow
it could become the nothing it is not.

The Moon You Are Creating

"The moon you are describing is the one
you are creating."
               —*William Stafford*

The beginning finds you
mapping out your sky,

searching unplowed star-fields
for rooted seas and woods.

While still a child, you notice
how the eye of night clouds over.

Days and weeks go by
before you see your pale hawk rise,

gyring round the world again,
bound—not blinded—by the earth,

as bright as the hour you feathered it.

Winter Geese

Sometimes I watch winter geese
veering back through dreams,

wild wings spread
like shadow-puppet hands,

lights above high desert dancing
behind a threadbare sheet.

From unmade beds
and ice-jammed fields, desire
ascends to heaven.

What use is it?

Roof-bound vanes shudder,
unwillingly point northwest

where clouds climb distant mountains,
trailing seed and mist.

Here in the parched morning,
earth swirls into dreadlocks
down an appaloosa's mane,

and wind rasps out
with a stutter—short of breath—
no answer to my question

put to sun and moon and rain.

WINTER CROWS

Again, the birds we take for omens,
for shadows slick as oil,
strut dissonance on yellow lawns.

Stiff-legged but winged,
they pitch and yaw through meager debris,
jostling the freeze-dried venom of fall.

Dawn unveils them ravening
after curbside scat, caw-quarreling
over autumn's carrion crumbs.

Feathers shine like blackened suns.
Feet score hieroglyphs
crisscross a cracked papyrus ground.

Outside my window, rapacious armies lunge.
But when I turn to find both crow and morning gone,
grass abandoned, early drafts undone,

I realize that, peck by peck, our ragged
world is drawn.

BARN SWALLOWS

On sun-singed feathers, water beads,
night leaves no mark, no telltale song
or bitter morning calling card.
Her tail's V flaunts a signal still forked,
her beak glares obsidian black.
I sweep her from the porch,
think twice and lumber down
to find her clutch of silence nesting
on glacial till's well-traveled stones.

Scooping her up, my hands mimic wings
as if each finger did not know
hands and wings prove never enough.
Suddenly her mate descends,
umbra burning like a flare across the wall,
curving in one lightning arc
to shadows glued between eave and roof.

Deep in feral grass, our house leans
toward unkempt forest,
toward oncoming thunderheads
as fierce as summer thorns.
Split and curled like madrona bark,
clapboard paint bares green over grey
over bones of riddled wood.
Beneath blackberry, cedar and Sitka Spruce,
clay rebounds another stubborn inch.

The Round Earth Theory

Earth is as old as you think her to be,
her islands gouged by famine,
her ocean edges rasped by war.

Gaia trembles when towers fall,
glaciers calve or mountains crumble.
As curved as scimitars, her corners are real.

Like her moon, Terra pales.
Healing will take more than
laying on of hands,
the whir of prayer wheels,
incessant smoke from corridors of candles.

Space itself bends back.
Blind light can only spiral down.
And isn't it a fact
that Raven circles till she drops,

searching for a scrap of meat,
a ball of dirt,
an unscarred skin of mud on which to strut?

String Theory

Simple as it seems, it can't be proven or dismissed.
Theories wax and wane like urban myths while we
repeat the same mistakes. You and I, let's say, fall
in and out of love again with memories and mist.
Not that we dispute the latest craze, a minor
genesis of miracles, big bangs and megabucks.

Total faith may leap while none-of-same falls flat, but
having neither, I stand unsure which foot to put before the other.
Either way, I'll find conundrums facing me
or chasing someone else. Dishes, dogs, talking heads, all
reverberate like violins. And the drone of the stars?
Yesterday's echo, a cry slow to fade from the brazen bull's throat.

II.

WOODCUTTER

Meadows open like goshawk wings.
Flower-feathered fields spread-eagle.
Sky stabs blue blades
through sleep's shuttered windows.
Your children wake.
Sun beats its moth-ringed body
free from the earth where you remain
splitting kindling and filling packs.
Laughter zigzags
like a bat dodging brooms,
reminding you how gravity
bends light like a spoon,
how paths once lit wind through black forest,
how crows stop quarreling to peck at crumbs.
Midday, you gather fallen fuel.
Evening, you argue with oncoming shadow.
When night knocks,
rolling thunder subsides to spells.
You stir your clutch of cackling coals,
then whirl with that dancer rising from wood.

DROUGHT

After a sleepless life, I find myself
exhausted from my trysts with coffee,
affairs with book, guitar and violin,
tempestuous marriage to poetry,
one-night stand with prayer.

I lift my green eyes for a sign,
for a dust-colored promise of roses,
torrents down the arroyo,
wadis flooded with dawn,
a phoenix bearing her body of ashes.

Memory circles beaten ground,
alights on cherry trees not yet in bloom.
Clouds of sparrows offer no shade,
but fields lie open to shifting wind,
to shadows which lengthen like omens.

Fear

The first nightmare
I dared to name was Raggedy Andy
shaking the bars on my bed.

I remember the knife gripped
high in his voice, as cold and white
as the saw-toothed stars
splayed on my smothering quilt.

I didn't know what dreams were.
I thought waking was death.

I thought light
would guide me through the world
if only I could hold it with my breath.

STICK MAN

The devil you know
trumps the devil you don't,
my grandmother loves to say.
But in my sleep, the goblin
refuses to scribble his name.

At the corner of Taylor and Lee,
where sidewalk tattoos lie salted and sanded
with mazes and spirals,
and burnished with Cambrian crumbs,
he unrolls his oilskin gaming cloth,
but because I've not yet mastered chess,
we settle for checkers instead.

Midway into our moonless match,
splinter fingers inch forward to cheat.
So from the grave-green parking strip
on which all dreamers meet,
I snatch a fallen ironwood branch,
and swing it as hard as I can.

I still hear the crack
as his arm snaps off
and drops like a staff to our street,
then, like a snake in rainstick forest,
rattles beyond my reach.

MIDDLE AGE

A zit blossoms like a moon,
pocking the center of my forehead.

Asleep, I am cradled
by unblemished hands.

Morning greets my third eye
as if it were a lover.

Sun says, "Welcome little chakra,
out-of-season flower!"

Unimpressed, mirror glares.
Not yet done with all my dreaming,

I blow gray snow
from the windy ridge of my razor.

What Raven Says

You will reach old age without spot.
You will sometimes think
what shouldn't be thought.
Your friends will be famous,
your appliances true. Your one
and only life? Half empty, half dull.
You will seldom win at tennis
but often lose at love.
You will retire to Arizona,
to hard yellow skies
where light from my agate-strewn islands
falls short of the stones
which will sleep on your eyes,
each one a black hand over jade-colored lies.

The Velocity of Autumn

In spite of red leaves, tart apples,
sharp cheddar cheese,
fall's loaded, illegal,
exceeding maximum tonnage.

Careening through orchards and cities,
one white-knuckled driver bears down,
blasting through straw-men,
showering sparks, triggering fire.

Gears grind, transmission screams
Ice! to no avail.
The cargo of curses shifts,
air-brakes rupture and fail.

Overblown, laden with ill,
autumn tilts, wails,
veers though unbanked hairpin turns,
then—end over clattering end—
tumbles down escarpments sopped in storms,
shrapnel from its shattered chassis
splintering shingles, severing limbs,
littering summer bazaars.

Skyward wheels unwind in the long unbroken night.
Timid stars like snow appear
as one remaining headlight glows.
We've missed our chance to run.
Entranced, we stand and stare,
rooted and riveted
like any startled deer.

BLACKBERRY HOUSE

Here is the house that earth worked
hard and long to buy, where ghosts
now board rent-free, where tangled August
pear trees shade crowns of berries.

Here is the mother who paid the bills,
the father whose ashes will never be found,
the boy whose balloon-tired bike
almost outran the elf-king's hound.

Here are the thorns which arch
across the yard, snagging strands of rain
from summer's low-slung clouds, poking fingers
under doors, invading the darkest rooms.

Here are the grids layered with mazes,
puzzles on puzzles, green worlds
in Gordian knots. How quickly vines
smother the grass. No blade can cut them back.

How surely they twine blood, ink and time
in fistfuls of tart black fruit.

TO A RUINED BUNKER STUMBLED INTO
WHILE EXPLORING FORT WORDEN STATE PARK

I too listen for the enemy,
my ear to the oiled air,
my black heart
clanking in its hole.

I too am brambled,
burrowed under skies of dirt,
my iron door shut,
my single eye scanning
the phantom fleet.

I too wish hard wishes of gravel,
heavy wishes of concrete:
that I might ring myself
with rusted barbs and greening briars,
that I might brood like a stone
set in water-sopped earth.

My brother, let us wait here together.

To My Left Hand

You, ring-bearer, the one
forced up behind my back,

the one not open, the one
two-faced like a feather

or a fist, the one cross-
wired to the wondrous flesh,

the one whose fingers
press the smooth dark neck

while the other pulls the bow.
The one unshaken,

the one held down
while the other salutes,

the one who slants this poem
to keep its blue-black ink

from smearing
like a streak of berry blood

across the wrist, the one
with claws, the one on fire,

the one they say
must lose its grip, the one

impertinent paw
whose palm remains

a revisable book, the twin
conjoined from birth

to the gypsy side of the heart.

AFTER LOOKING AT A FACSIMILE OF LEONARDO'S JOURNALS,

I tried but failed to copy this poem from right
to left, each difficult letter facing backwards.
I hope that you, now peering through

the other side, forgive my semi-awkward gestures.
Toward you, I hold no sinister intent,
imaginary reader. You are different from the nine-

out-of-ten leading right-handed lives, from those haughty
few staring out with leveled eyes from ambidextrous houses.
If difficulties arise, I apologize.

You and I have flipped our images as many times
as we've rearranged furniture, remade our beds, or revised
x-rated drafts of our unpublished lives.

While we may someday emerge from obscurity with reversed
graffiti sprawled like angels across trompe l'oeil ceilings,
I'm afraid we'll never get our naked figures right.

THE DEVELOPING TRAY

A thousand drops of rain
poised mid-burst on a pockmarked street

float beside firecrackers
caught mid-crack by an almost silent click.

Flickering light, sculpted smoke,
the alchemy of space

distills itself in black-and-white.

Supernovas—time-bending roses
shrunk to the size of pre-engorged ticks—

swim beside close-ups of a rotting peach

which the sewer-sweetened tongues of critic mice
find good enough to eat.

VILLAGE OF THE MERMAIDS

after the painting by Paul Delvaux

Together, the women sit alone,
their eyes like those of air-

drowned fish, their long hair
fashioned into ripples

reminiscent of a spawning river's
troubled falls.

A distant man, neither harem eunuch
nor fleeing groom,

skirts the sky-colored sea.
He does not doff his weathered hat;

nor does he allow the viewer
a voyeur's glimpse of his face.

He just tip-toes away in silent cat boots
from the stinking sight of us.

TAKE MAGRITTE

for example. He sees an egg
but paints a bird. He paints himself
ogling the egg while painting the bird.
He pictures himself eating the egg
while dreaming the bird.
In another life the bird returns.
She is nothing
but a hole in the bird-shaped sky.
And Magritte? He's green as a feather.
He's an apple an inch from your eye.

Take me. I see him painting a pipe.
He writes, "This is not a pipe,"
under the painted pipe. I write
within the poem, "This is not a poem,"
though it must ring true if it curves,
has a clapper, and isn't a bell.
Take Magritte again. I see him in a room
with his painted brush and comb. He writes,
"This is not a room; this is not death; this is
not about a poem."

LANDSCAPE WITH VIOLIN

Breakfast done, I slip outside
to practice and to play.

My bow and violin,
which, in secret, I set down,
lie quiet as rosin dust
yellowing our lawn.

Before my mother calls me in,
I lift them up; and for a moment
whitening with dawn,

I see an outline pressed in grass:
shoulders, hips—
the perfect violin.

Night fades again
as blades unbend
like monks released from prayer
when a golden gong is rung.

.

INSTRUMENTS

The feet, the hands, the arrogant hips,
the long thigh bones,
none of these, none of these
dance alone.

They hum like ignorant cellos,
clash like deaf steel drums.

When steel rusts and wood's unstrung,
when the dance master's gone,
who in the world will dance with them?

The sky? The wind?
Our whirling earth?
The legs of the strutting sun?

To a Pawned Guitar

Your rain songs fall
quiet as light
fingering fretted streams.

Your snow songs float
white as ash
silencing raucous skies.

Your space songs empty
immensity
of all unneeded things.

I think you think
I have washed my hands
of your cold, metal strings.

To a Slinky

On stairs that
drop to our hall,

necessity
draws you thin.

Are you ribless
spine & tail,

or rippled
waterfall?

Momentum
carries you down

accordion
whorls of sound.

Gravity grins.
Solemnity spins.

Loop after loop
descends.

At the Symphony

Between the warring
archipelagos of sound,

reeds revolt.

A movement swelling
like a young sequoia sprouts.

Songs and canyons open to

rapid beats of goshawk wings.
Thunder follows;

yet silence remains

a perfect surface shattered by
arpeggios of no one's dreams.

ELEGY FOR A BORDER COLLIE

Yes, I reply to the cryptic stones,
she was the alpha pup
who refused to grow up,
more human
than my snarly neighbors.

She reveled in necessity:
herding cats, scolding geese,
disturbing the high-and-mighty
fortresses of squirrels.

And yes, she would have tumbled
like one of you
down the salmon's icy ladders,
or levitated over embers
to catch her Frisbee had I asked.

Divining the weather ahead,
she suffered critic crows,
and gathered out of fall's debris
a whirling litter of her own.

Now her doe eyes target spinning suns,
and her wolf ears perk at howling moons.
She runs, leaps, zeros in
where I will not, cannot
call her home.

North of the Crater

Sometimes water falls
with hints of cedar, fir and spruce—

promises whispered
against tympanums of mist.

Other times silence and ash
attempt once more to inundate our tracks.

Whatever the course or cost of weather,
science can only guess

how many dreams must pass
before Crow sets sail from her battered branch,

before earth's grave
thirst is quenched,

and mud again conceives
conspiracies as confident as grass.

North of Hatteras

While we sat sipping nectar
from a goblet at the Pearl,
staring down our measured ocean
never silent in the face of love,

we didn't notice dusk
crash forward into dawn,
old arguments still polishing
smooth stones.

And when we taught our wishful skin
to dance and swim,
we didn't see time strobing
outward on its ripple,
splashing over troubled fields.

We only saw the warm wine
blooming from its pedestal—
a moment's blur of shadow and of sun.

We only noticed late day soften
before the moon again
bore witness, then rowed on.

Nowhere

Ship horns ooze slow sound today,
cruel, malevolent, oily.
Smears of grey, wolfish light
erase cliffs, and I can't recall
where the corniche curves
or the walk runs laser-straight.
Cedars anchoring soil to stars disappear.
Wet blades adhere to bare flesh and feet.
All night the fog pressed down
its chloroformed rag.
A trawler faded, a tanker burned,
each greasing the edge of saber-sharp reefs.
Morning finds me facing blank screens,
as lost as I was in unmuzzled sun
before clouds inched east
over old-growth spruce, and the mute tide
swaddled our roughshod beach.

Dream of the Savanna

Baggage lost, rains wrung dry,
stories scoured by whims of air,
I arrive a stranger

worn thin by voyaging,
by wondering and warring,
by my tribe's sixty-thousand-year march.

Has my scroll of rivers
unwound to its end?
I ask, but no one living knows.

The map to my village?
Nowhere found.
Grandmother elephant refuses to say

where she has carried
the bones of my name.
Baobab's broad back shields me from sun

while wind-through-tall-grass
whispers, *Here!*, but whirls on.

Disturbing the Universe

Between two shafts of light,
I lift a stone

from underneath the waterfall,
drop its weight

with wondering hands
into a pocket of my jeans,

then speed my burning engine home
over twilight's broken roads.

After raking water's gift of sand
into orbits ringing once wet worlds,

I dance on the drome of the revving rain
revising arroyos for rivers to dream.

BEAVERTON, OREGON BLUES

When there is no wind, rain
tells vertical stories about the ground.

Like waterlogged boots
left out on the lawn, cedar and pine
stand soaked with silence.

When sky scuttles by on sand or sound,
grey sighs muffle the green river's song.

Threadbare firs line up—
all my poor relations—as I slog away
from the Hall Street Grill.

Today I caulked another poem.
Or was it a boat, a window, a room?

When little sparks speak
like newborn suns,
we douse our steaming houses down.

The Sun Again

The sun again glares down
our drying sea of guttered streets
the first time this side
of many muddied weeks.

Accustomed to our filtered light,
we dare not stare him in his face.
We wear brimmed hats,
draw down blinds, squint
through shades and tinted glass.

But when the long clouds
congregate in rows
as dark-redundant as cathedral pews,
we dart outdoors—*umbrellas up*—
pretend he never came.

We know each story worth our wait
is written in the rain.

Logos

Like rain from slate-gray sky,
words congregate in pools,
then carve the quickest downhill cut
toward any rumor of shore.

Once spoken, they return to air,
leaving on lake beds cracked clay
with white scrawlings of salt.

Rising to descend, they sink
to well from rock.
Thunder is with them—ice, boulders,
wreckage of arks.

Gouging arroyos through black basalt,
they prove dangerous
when dammed like rivers

or left alone like paper-thin frost.

Thirst

A tree made only
of stars
towers above us.

You:
half a drop
of water;

me:
infinitesimal,
dry—

no thing
but a thought
rattling in an atom,

no ocean
but this notion
split open like a seed.

III.

Irregularities in the White

suggest a field of snow
    or snow falling
        soft
            as a veil
on the seventh night.

The way light
    from my window strikes
        the vast
            and empty page
is the way
    light touches ice,

        the way ice seals
            for a time
the mouth of the earth.

But something
    tiny as a vole
        leaves hesitant tracks,

something sudden
    as an owl
        drops to circle back,

and within the shadows
    lie
        the shadows
of a right and left hand.

OLD STORY

They say that God was telling
her unbelievable story
when suddenly she pulled
a slender hand full of props
(sun, moon, earth and various stars)
from her sky-black velvet purse.
After setting each
in almost perfect motion,
she paused
while creation held its breath
for the inescapable conclusion.

None of this matters to you or me.
Philosophy won't clear arteries
or send blood coursing through thought.
And when you think
you have it nailed down,
wind shifts and shadows sharpen—
a heron ripples mirror's pond;
a goshawk drops without a sound.

LETTER TO MEISTER ECKHART

On moonless nights
when your body is nothing
but a burl
scarring its wooden bed,
do you imagine
the author of all throbbing things
would hesitate to show himself
as fire within the waterfall,
as flames cascading
down crimson cloaks of magic
morning glories?

Could he be that dancing dwarf,
shape-shifting king
web-footing
even as we speak
among the leaves and lily pads,
blindsided
by the shimmer and spell,
skipping like a moss-winged stone
over widening rings of wonder?

Under a Japanese Maple

As I attempt to tidy up our yard,
the one thing I forgot

pokes through my mind
like a stalk of saw-toothed prairie

through a concrete walk,
a fist sucker-punched through a wall.

It's useless to complain.
Shapeshifters never stop.

Sleek as jackdaws, quiet as cats,
they lie in wait like spring-loaded traps

triggered by nothing
but a feather or a leaf—

from the first fallen fire to the last red raked.

MIDNIGHT IN THE GARDEN

In this as yet undreamed of tale,
I am not bilingual.
Half your dying language
proves enough.

But you might ask me
why I then wear sheaths of stars
around the teardrop
of my pale blue back-lit pearl?

So I argue for the other side,
swallow words, shed my tail.

I teach my golden tongue to fork
before it greets two perfect strangers
free to quarrel

over who shall gather, who shall hunt,
who shall sow—hands black with ink—
the blood-dark maize and bulgur wheat
in this as yet uncostumed tale.

GARTER SNAKES

Curled in a nave of the garden,
    born live in the ruins of the choir,
how lucky are her young,
    how blessed.

In the quarry, they slip
    between stones, whisper
 in tracery tongues
    as cool and ancient as moss.

They wake to the first
    or final kiss of whatever wisp
leans over their nest.
    From half-closed fists

they stare with eyes almost
    like ours. We see their hunger,
moist as a tendril,
    unfurl toward fragile light.

How eager they appear,
    in coils of their mother,
to swallow whole
    our cloudless weather

where blood, as innocent as lightning,
    and as cold as any stream
within the mountains or the mind,
    beckons with its still, small voice.

THE PETRIFIED WIFE

Around her circle ravenous gulls,
    bone of a moon, red-
shifting stars. Wind and rain
    erode copper hair. Sleet
pocks once translucent skin.
    While horse, deer and fox
lick salt from her feet,
    she dreams day and night
of houses aflame,
    of blizzard-thick ash
swaddling her grief.
    Were it possible to speak,
conceivable to wake, what then?
    She cannot quiet salacious crows,
quench mineral tears,
    roll stones from dead tongues.
The moment she blinked,
    scuttling leaves froze.
When she was a girl,
    when she was a wife,
when she played trick-or-treat,
    when she turned for a last
quick glance at her life. . .

WATER PLANET

The day Noah died,
mourners burned gopher wood,
raven and dove made salty love,
ashes wandered eroded sky.

As mindless as Sahara wind,
monsoons rippled sound and stream.
The Tigris offered gifts of fish
to cities schooling in her womb.

Ganges, Nooksack, Nile and Snake
bore woven cradles caulked with grief
which journey on—nightlights lit—
like paper boats toward unknown reefs.

Pangaea's embers drift like pollen
on broken images of sun.
Where currents quicken, sparks follow
the pull of dolphin moons.

Again and again the soft stars sleep.
Again we wake to know
our old, unquenchable stories
swarm like minnows through new bones.

Running in D.C.

After reading a review of
A Brief History of Time, the book
one critic labels
"most likely to remain unfinished,"
I jog in Rock Creek Park.

I follow the black stream, its surface
littered with flotsam and jetsam,
the pirated gimcracks of autumn.

Before my few miles end, I'm struck by
how effortlessly our universe expands
into oblivion.
It too outpaces me.

Step after step interrupts my fall
as I near Adams Mill
where, in the distance, signals shift,
allowing star-filled flumes to flow.

Slippery rivers—suddenly pale—
spill from blades of well-oiled wheels.

KINDERGARTEN: 1945

We learn to name three colors
sewn onto flags, and six hues
oozing from rainbows.
Our word-of-the-day is *atom*.
In the half-life of school,
we are taught to look straight ahead.
I fidget and scribble mandalas—
spinning and sprawling
Crack-the-Whip worlds.
With powder-paint and crayons,
I am God. In dug-out forts, I rule.
But Miss Bell's words crater my dirt.
Art is never practical.

Under gilded dragons at the Capitol Theater,
tsunamis circle our black-and-white Earth.
Bodies bob like bloated seals,
tumble like cordwood
before blades of bulldozers.
Awed by its burden of color,
I watch *The Wizard of Oz*. For now,
I am spared the mountains of gold.
For now, I am spared.

On streets half-lit with winter,
I play soldier with a toy German Luger.
At home, I practice the violin.
Because I am small, my grandmother
helps me hold up its neck
by sticking my elbow, as it wavers again,
with an exquisitely rendered,
unbendable pin.

Vaudeville at the Palomar

The last full-time vaudeville theater in America,
demolished in the mid-20th Century to make room
for a post office and parking garage.

At the age of six, I believed
the tuxedoed magician as he sawed
two naked legs—soon twenty feet
downstage and kicking—
from the screaming upper-half
of his blindingly blond assistant.
I wept when, on its own, each thigh,
ankle and tapping toe returned.
I believed as I heard the memory-man
rattle names of every soul
from box to balcony backwards.
I believed the memory-man's wink
turned to tongue, turned to whisper
in my mother's ear
the moment she shook his hand.

I believe the memory-man is de facto
defunct, the Palomar's last act
was Sammy Davis Jr., and postal workers
will someday serve everyone in line
from drunks at Third and University
to stiffs on Pike and Pine.

High School

Not for girls too tall
Not for boys too short
Not for girls too fat
Not for boys too dumb
Not for girls too gangly
Not for boys too poor
Not for girls with foreign names
Not for boys with allergies
Not for girls with two left feet
Not for boys with warts
Not a place to share your secrets
Not a place to bare your soul
Not a place you'd want to live
Not a laughing matter
Not the diploma nailed to your wall
Not the Buddha
Not the Christ
Not where you find the love of your life
Not that anyone cares

The Farewell

Already, oaks loom between us,
though I have not yet crossed the first hill.
Sky curls up like a grey-muzzled dog.
White noise hardens into ice. Knives
jangle from the frozen fingertips of pines.
One key clicks. A needle sticks
in scratched repeating vinyl riffs.
No jingling ghosts or wooden angels speak.
No coloratura breezes lisp.

Broken gates awake as wind
ushers me past house and barn
toward blackened cloudbanks calving storms.
Hands vanish into pockets. Hardwoods
ring a crackling wall around my father's fields.

GHOST

In my dream there's a hole
cut from sky, a hole
sliced from beating sky,
a hole in the shape of my father.
If he comes to me, will I know him?
Will he pass like a quark
through the veil of my skin
or read me to sleep
from my favorite book?
If he comes to me, will I know him?
Will I know from new ink
on my untouched brush, or from breath
shared between storms?
Will I know by a smile or an ignorant stare?
If he knocks, will I ask him in?

From a Lost Album

The past is still, for us, a place
that is not safely settled.
        —Michael Ondaatje

He's one blade of prairie
pressed flat in a dream, this stranger
with narrow face and mismatched eyes
that dance askance like mine.
In my hand, he mirrors my young son's gaze.

Six weeks west from Illinois,
on rations of jerky and beans,
he won't meet Rachel or marry Claire,
but he'll board the train.
He's standing by the blue-black engine
that always leaves on time.

Seven days from Seattle, he'll buy a bride.
Three of five children will toughen and bloom.
Like weeds on sod roofs
letting rainwater slide,
they'll riddle our walls with roots.

SLEEPING ON AMTRAK

Evening slathers borrowed gold
on strangers' faces,

drops a skin of rain
on fields and silos streaming by.

A faint click-clack with shadows
fans shuttered eyes.

Towns recede like memories of kisses,
broken toys, first snow, seventh grade.

Tracks tunnel into haze
enveloping a trestle over mocha river veins.

Loosely worn by summer,
dusk's threadbare veil caresses us,

as fragile as the fog that shelters lovers,
as quick to vanish as

one-hundred years of steam.

Letter to a Lost Brother

Forget about the weather
and whether or not the two of us
threw sticks and stones,
or spat words at childhood's bones.

Bribe an angel, tap a message,
smuggle out a sign.
Silence is the granite
I'd roll back from your grave.

In case you don't know, I'm older,
the world's warming,
and we're not on standard time.
In case you care, I'll stay awake

burning this letter
in some windless recess of my brain,
burning till, through the smoke,
your distant planet shines.

THE PICNIC

from an old, family photograph

There are no gods combing the beach
yet the clan dresses as if at church,

the men in bowler hats and starched shirts,
the women cinched in summer heat.

Tradition or respect?
The day, long gone, demands a guess.

Among them, my mother's mother,
her raven spirit at its best.

Persistent as the shuffling surf,
her life-long prayer repeats

one cloudless Sunday morning
on the shore of Dungeness Spit.

For a moment, she stands among them,
resplendent in ruffles and pleats.

There is no death as far as she can see,
only tea, cookies and cinnamon cakes,

and wave after wave like ribbons
as far as the wind can snake.

ARCHAEOLOGY

Because your soil is spiked
with mainland memory and island dreams,
you grasp the green moraine
with mattock, claw, and leather gloves.

You find a ring, a lidless jar
that once held coins, letters bearing
legends of your spirit name.

A vessel surfaces—translucent china
cormorant divining up through dirt.
You hear your father's ghost
calling from your mother's mind,
from the center of a lake long silted up.
It's never enough.

You find twigs but not the mandrake root,
no skull-tipped key to hidden doors
or click of magic metal forcing your dead to talk.
But you go on digging.

Before light fades, you hope to tap
the unspoiled tomb. When earth offers you
a cup of cold water, you drink
from the leaking cradle of your hands—
to now and to the severed sod
drying in the sun

Dropcloth

The pharaohs gathered daytime
treasure into lightless tombs,

never to reflect one ray of Ra,
never to be viewed

by those who have not rowed
Nun's barque of moonless dreams.

But at my wakeful feet today, a jar
lies broken—the one I threw

to hold spare change,
to prop up pencils, brushes, roses,

my tools-of-trade, my burning fuses,
a pauper's objects of desire.

Imagine my surprise to find
the inside outside,

a gutted geode spewing blue,
its fire-fused cataract—once intact—

now half my lifetime splashed across
the dropcloth in our sunlit cave.

Tunnel Vision

The hole is bottomless,
or so it seems.
We toss the first stone in—

no sound returns.
What spirits rise
fade with a flutter of wings.

We imagine magma's
vacant rooms,
obsidian spirals,

onyx domes.
We descend for hours,
or so it seems,

strung together like beads,
the lamps on our helmets
like red-shifting suns,

our feet flaring like hands.
Dream after dream
drops lifelines down.

We measure silence
on a gong of water.
We join the black stream.

When our slender
passage narrows,
we lengthen into worms.

In darkness, we remember
noon, light's thin fingers
under doors,

dust lit up like angels
in shafts of fluted air.
Only then do we break through,

turn root-rugged ceilings
into floors, squint again
at far flung stars—

Andromeda,
Canopus,
Rigel Kentaurus—

each spark a grain
of shotgunned gold
salting midnight's choirs.

ABOUT THE AUTHOR

Paul Fisher was born and grew up in Seattle, and graduated from Queen Anne High School, that haunted institution which is now a historical landmark. He earned a master's degree in Art & Education from Washington University in St. Louis, an MFA in poetry from New England College, and has studied writing in a variety of academic and workshop settings, including the University of Washington, the Centrum Foundation, and the Writer's Center in Bethesda, Maryland. The recipient of an Individual Artist's Fellowship in Poetry from the Oregon Arts Commission, he has moved into and out of more parts of the country than he cares to think about. Visual artist as well as poet, he believes that poetry has as much in common with music and painting as it has with prose. Paul lives in Bellingham, Washington with his wife, Linda. His poems have appeared in dozens of periodicals and in several anthologies. *Rumors of Shore*, the winner of the 2009 Blue Light Book Award, is his first book.

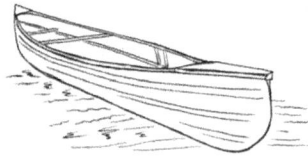

Printed in the United States of America